To my loving husband
who constantly reminds
me that it isn't always
about catching a fish.

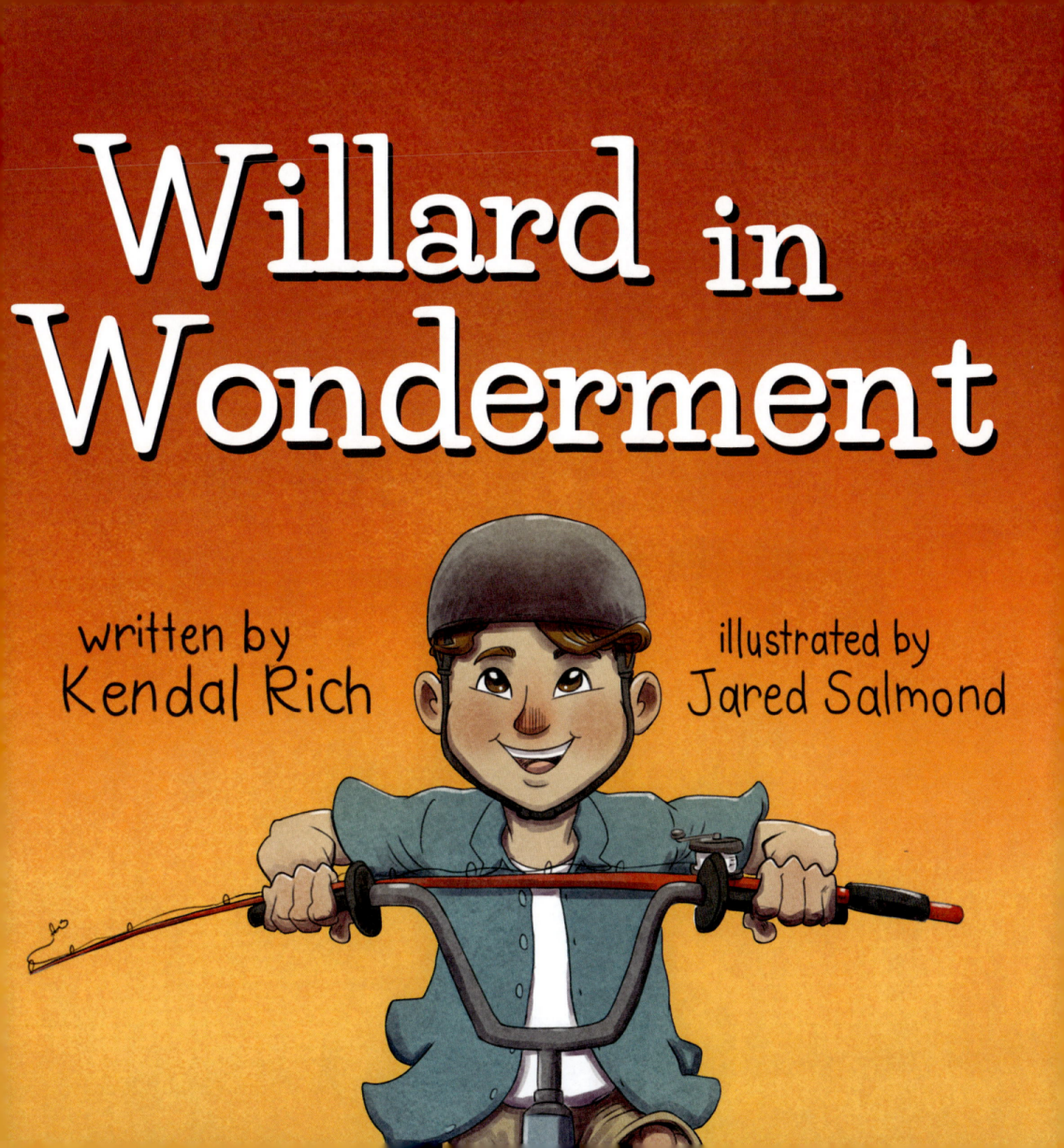

Willard spent his days near lakes and rivers, hoping to catch a fish. Each day, Willard rode his bike to a pond by his house. Before getting on his bike, Willard would tie his shoes into tangled knots so that they wouldn't get caught in his bike chain.

One day when Willard went to the pond, he cast his line into the water and then sat on a tree stump and eagerly waited. He waited a long time, and didn't catch anything. When the sun began to set, he knew it was almost time for dinner, and headed home.

Disappointed, he asked Mom, "Why can't I catch any fish?"

"Willard, you've caught a lot of fish before, but this is a hard time of year for fishing. The fish are really cold so they don't want to move much. When you don't catch anything, what do you do?"

Willard shrugged and said, "I just wait."

"Do you ever just sit and look at the sky, the sunset or the reflection of the big mountains in the water?" asked Mom. Willard shook his head. Mom added, "You know those paintings you do in art class?" Willard nodded.

"Have you ever thought about the pond as a painting created just for you?" asked Mom.

Willard sat and thought for a minute.

In a huff, Willard stood up and said, "I don't know, Mom. I just want to catch a fish!" He stomped off to his bedroom.

"Goodnight, Willard, I love you," replied Mom.

The next day, Willard visited his Grandpa. He loved visiting Grandpa because he always told exciting adventure stories. Grandpa grew up on the beaches of California, where the waves would splash his feet and baby sand crabs would tickle his toes in the sand. He would always tell Willard tales of his deep-sea fishing adventures. He caught all kinds of fish, big and small.

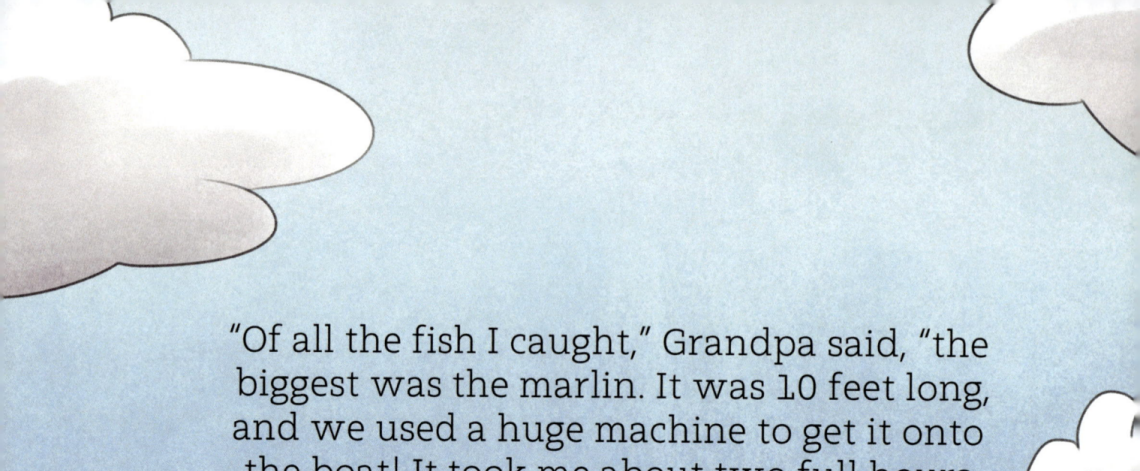

"Of all the fish I caught," Grandpa said, "the biggest was the marlin. It was 10 feet long, and we used a huge machine to get it onto the boat! It took me about two full hours to tire it out and reel it in."

Willard was amazed by Grandpa's catch and knew if he wanted to catch a fish, Grandpa could help him.

Willard asked, "Grandpa, can I tell you something?"

"Of course, Willard. What is it?"

"Well, I haven't caught a fish in a really long time, but I really, really want to."

"That's okay," Grandpa replied. "I remember many times not catching one either. I'd sit on the shore and watch the surfers ride big waves, or admire the beautiful sunsets. I spent a lot of time waiting and admiring the world around me. Often those were my favorite times. That's when I felt true ***wonderment***."

Willard folded his arms and stomped his foot.
"Ugh… but I'm done waiting!"

"I know it's hard, but really look around
next time you are out there. You might be
surprised by what you see."

Willard felt frustrated that Grandpa didn't give him some kind of secret to catching fish. But with that frustration came a determination to finally catch one of his own. He got his fishing pole, knotted his shoes, and raced to the pond as the sun started to set. He cast his line into the water and sat on the same stump, and waited.

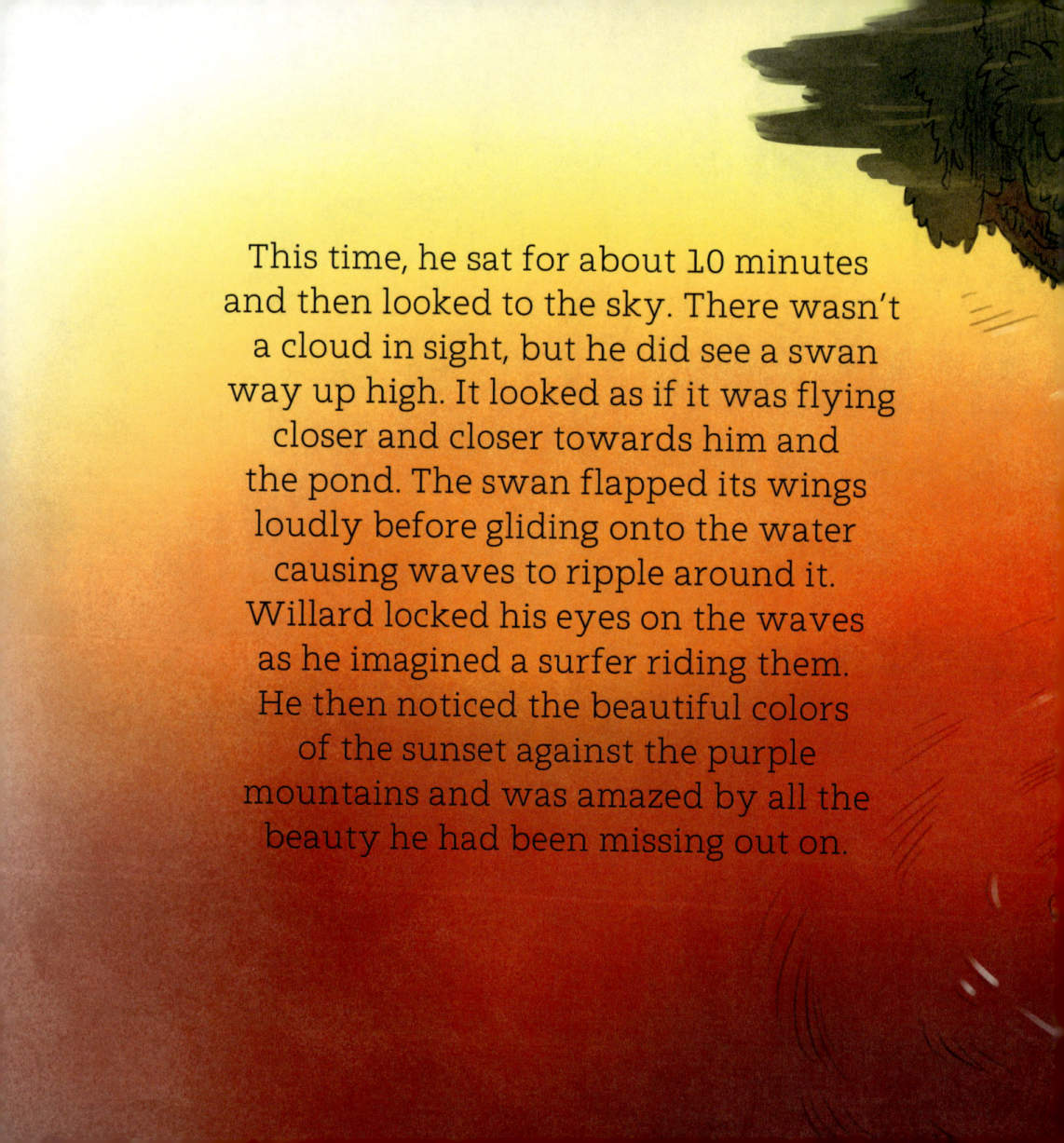

*This must be the **wonderment** Grandpa was talking about,* Willard thought. Before he knew it, the sun had completely set. With a smile, he packed up his things and rode home. When he got there, his mom was waiting with dinner.

"Thank you for dinner, Mom," Willard grinned.

"Did you catch your fish?" she asked.

"Nope," he replied, shaking his head. "But I saw that painting you were talking about. Also, can you show me how to tie my shoes again?"

"Of course, honey," she said with a laugh. As she got up to help him with his shoes, she added,

"One day you will catch your fish Willard, but until then, there will always be **wonderment**."

ABOUT THE AUTHOR

Kendal grew up on the beaches of Southern California, but now resides in Utah with her husband Gavin where they enjoy fishing, hunting, and camping in the majestic mountains. The first book she authored was "Through the Muds in Mexico", which she wrote while studying English and Professional Writing at Brigham Young University. Her latest published works are Children's Books titled "Fred the Oversized Watermelon" and "We Are All Trees."

You can follow her and her adventures on Instagram @kendalrich23

If you liked this book, give it a review on Amazon!

Made in the USA
Middletown, DE
27 May 2024

54893289R00015